THE
TOTALLY
CARROT
COOKBOOK

THE
TOTALLY
CARROT
COOKBOOK

By Helene Siegel & Karen Gillingham
Illustrated by Carolyn Vibbert

CELESTIAL ARTS
BERKELEY, CALIFORNIA

The Totally Carrot Cookbook is produced
by becker&mayer!, Ltd.
Kirkland, Washington.
www.beckermayer.com

Printed in Singapore.

Cover design and illustration: Bob Greisen
Interior design: Susan Hernday
Interior illustrations: Carolyn Vibbert
Typesetting: Matt Hutnak

Library of Congress Cataloging-in-Publication Data
Siegel, Helene.
        The totally carrot cookbook / by Helene Siegel &
    Karen Gillingham.
        p. cm.
    ISBN 0-89087-948-6 (pbk.)
    1. Cookery (Carrots) I. Gillingham, Karen. II. Title.
TX803.C35S54 2000
641.6′513--dc21   99-42007
                                             CIP

Celestial Arts Publishing
P.O. Box 7123
Berkeley, CA 94707

Look for all 32 *Totally* books at your local store!

TO PETER RABBIT

CONTENTS

INTRODUCTION

Why cook a carrot? Recently, I bit into a sample offered by a grower at my local farmers market, and it gave way to my teeth with a crunchy snap, and tasted so sweet I wondered why carrots aren't candy instead of vegetables.

But there are good reasons to cook a carrot. Another farmer at the market told me how he makes soup: Steam a bunch of carrots, purée them in the blender, add salt to taste. That's it—although sometimes he adds a few beets, the only vegetable with a higher sugar content than carrots.

The carrot is an aromatic vegetable, which means it lends its rich, sweet nature to everything it touches—other vegetables, a cut-up chicken, a hearty pot roast, a cup of rice, a cake with fragrant spices, or a complex stock.

Indeed, a *mirepoix*, a mixture of diced carrots, onions, and celery, is a staple of French-trained cooks who use it to flavor sauces, soups, and stews, as well as for a bed on which to roast meat.

Happily, baby carrots, as well as water-packed grated and cut forms, are now readily available in most markets. Unlike cooking green vegetables, you have to practically burn a carrot before its color will fade. That bright orange color comes from beta-carotene, one of the highly stable pigments that give fruits and vegetables like canteloupes and squash their color. A precursor to vitamin A, beta-carotene is also the star nutrient in carrots. And cooking makes this nutrient more usable by the body. Hopefully, you'll find more good reasons to cook carrots as you turn the pages that follow. Then there's the matter of bunnies. Bugs Bunny is always shown firmly gripping a green-topped carrot. *The Runaway Bunny* ends happily with a carrot reward, and one popular carrot packager calls itself Bunny-Luv. Yet while researching Beatrix Potter to pepper this text with Peter Rabbit quotes, I found no mention of carrots. Peter stuffed himself with lettuces and parsley and other things green. I asked the soup-making farmer why Peter Rabbit never ate a carrot. "Rabbits eat carrot tops, not the orange root," he said. Maybe. I say Mrs. Rabbit's naughty little boy passed up the best thing in Mr. McGregor's garden. So, Peter, this book is for you.

CARROTS
FOR
COCKTAILS

MARINATED BABY CARROTS WITH CUMIN

Serve these with toothpicks...and martinis, perhaps?

½ pound baby carrots
1 tablespoon sugar
¼ cup extra virgin olive oil
1 tablespoon white wine vinegar
1 garlic clove, minced
1 tablespoon chopped fresh parsley
½ teaspoon crushed cumin seeds
pinch red pepper flakes
salt

In a small saucepan with enough water to cover, bring carrots, sugar, and water to a boil. Reduce heat and simmer 5 minutes. Drain.

In a bowl, whisk together olive oil with vinegar. Whisk in garlic, parsley, cumin, pepper flakes, and salt to taste. Toss carrots into the mixture, cover, and chill. Serve cold.

SERVES 4

CARROT ASPARAGUS TERRINE

For an elegant dinner party, serve slices over lettuce leaves, or serve more casually with toasted baguette slices.

2 cups carrots boiled, steamed, or
    microwaved, and mashed
2 cups ½-inch asparagus lengths
1 cup dry bread crumbs
½ cup shredded Gruyère cheese
¼ cup minced shallots
4 eggs, lightly beaten
⅛ teaspoon cayenne pepper
salt

Preheat oven to 350 degrees F. Butter bottom and sides of a 9- x 5-inch loaf pan.

In a large bowl, combine carrots, asparagus, bread crumbs, cheese, shallots, eggs, and cayenne. Mix well. Season to taste with salt. Pour into the prepared pan. Set the pan in a larger baking pan, and pour in hot water to come halfway up the loaf pan. Cover with foil, and bake about 1 hour or until a knife inserted in the center comes out clean. Cool on a wire rack, then chill overnight. Turn out, slice, and serve.

SERVES 6

"Carrots are underground honey."
        —Irish expression

SPICY CARROT AND SWEET POTATO DIP

For dipping, cut pita bread into wedges, then toast in 325-degree-F oven until golden.

1 pound carrots, cut in 1-inch chunks
½ pound sweet potatoes, peeled and cut in
  1-inch chunks
2 garlic cloves, roughly chopped
1½ teaspoons ground cumin
½ teaspoon ground coriander
¼ teaspoon cayenne pepper
3 tablespoons extra virgin olive oil
2 tablespoons balsamic vinegar
salt
pita chips or crudités

In a large saucepan, bring carrots and sweet potatoes to a boil in enough water to cover. Reduce heat, and simmer 15 minutes or until vegetables are soft. Drain. Transfer to a food processor, and add garlic, cumin, coriander, cayenne, oil, and vinegar. Process until puréed. Season to taste with salt. Serve warm with pita chips.

SERVES 8

Size Matters

Larger carrots are often sweeter than skinny ones. Huge carrots, however, should be avoided: they are less tasty and have woody cores.

MEXICAN PICKLED CARROTS

At Mexican restaurants in Southern California, fiery pickled vegetables such as these are placed on the table as a relish.

3 cups ¼-inch-thick carrot slices
1 cup cauliflowerets
3 tablespoons olive oil
½ onion, thinly sliced
2 garlic cloves, roughly chopped
1 cup white wine vinegar
1 bay leaf
½ teaspoon dried oregano
8 peppercorns
½ teaspoon salt
1 (6½-ounce) can whole jalapeños (not
   pickled)

Cook carrots and cauliflower in boiling salted water to cover, 3 minutes. Drain.

In a medium saucepan, heat oil over medium-high heat. Sauté onion and garlic, stirring frequently, until onion is soft, about 3 minutes. Stir in vinegar, bay leaf, oregano, peppercorns, and salt. Simmer 5 minutes. Stir in jalapeño peppers, carrots, and cauliflower. Bring to a boil, then remove from heat and allow to cool. Cover, and refrigerate for at least two days before serving.

MAKES ABOUT 1½ QUARTS

Carrot Kin

Fresh green carrot tops can be chopped and added to soups and salads just as you would use parsley, the carrot's cousin. Then there's Uncle Dill and Aunt Parsnip.

DILLED CARROT CHIPS

Bet you can't eat just one!

vegetable oil for deep-frying
large carrots
dried dill
salt

In a deep fryer or large pot, heat about 4 inches of oil to 365 degrees F.

With a vegetable peeler, cut long, thin strips as wide as possible from carrots. Drop a few at a time into hot oil. Fry just until crisp, about 20 seconds. Drain on paper towels, and sprinkle with dill and salt.

SERVES 2 PER CARROT

COLORFUL
SOUPS
AND
SALADS

GINGERED CARROT SOUP

Serve in shallow bowls or mugs.

2 tablespoons butter
1 small onion, chopped
1 celery stalk, chopped
2 teaspoons minced fresh ginger
¾ pound carrots, roughly chopped
2 tablespoons flour
4 cups vegetable or chicken broth
salt and freshly ground pepper
1 teaspoon grated orange zest

In a large saucepan, melt butter over medium heat. Sauté onion, celery, and ginger until softened, about 5 minutes. Stir in carrots and sprinkle evenly with flour. Cook and stir 1 minute longer. Stir in broth and bring to a boil. Reduce to a simmer, cover, and cook 30 minutes. Transfer to a blender, and purée in batches until smooth. Season with salt and pepper to taste. Sprinkle with orange zest, and serve hot.

SERVES 4

"The day is coming when a single carrot freshly observed [in a painting] will set off a revolution."
      —*Paul Cézanne*

CARROT VICHYSSOISE

This classic cold summer soup gets a face-lift when you substitute carrots for the traditional potatoes.

4 cups roughly chopped carrots
3 leeks, white part only, sliced
4 cups chicken or vegetable broth
juice and grated zest of 1 orange
1 cup half-and-half
salt and white pepper
sour cream, chopped chives or fresh dill, and
    orange-peel twists for garnish

In a large saucepan, combine carrots, leeks, and broth. Bring to a boil. Reduce heat, and simmer uncovered 25 minutes or until vegetables are tender. Transfer in batches to a blender, and process until puréed.

Transfer to a large bowl, and stir in juice, orange zest, and half-and-half. Season to taste with salt and pepper. Chill. Serve in bowls, garnished with sour cream, chives, and orange-peel twists.

SERVES 6

20/20

The ancients believed carrots strengthened eyesight, and rightly so. The orange color of the root is produced by beta-carotene, which improves our ability to see in dim light. It is also an antioxidant important to keeping our skin healthy.

CREAM OF CARROT SOUP WITH DILL

You can use the food processor to chop the carrots since they will eventually be puréed. This formula makes an elegant creamed soup out of any of your favorite root vegetables.

2 tablespoons butter
1 onion, sliced
1 teaspoon salt
1 bunch fresh dill
4 cups chicken broth
1 pound carrots, finely chopped
2 cups half-and-half
salt and freshly ground pepper, to taste

In a large, heavy pot, melt butter over low heat. Cook onion with salt until soft, about 5 minutes.

Divide dill in half and tie stems together with kitchen string. Pick off leaves and reserve for garnish. Add dill stems and chicken broth to the pot. Bring to a boil and cook over moderate heat 15 minutes. Remove, and discard the dill stems. Add the carrots. Bring to a boil, return to a simmer, and cook uncovered until the carrots are soft, about 10 minutes.

Transfer to a food processor or blender, and purée until smooth. Strain back into the pot, pressing with a wooden spoon to extract the juices. Pour in the half-and-half, bring to a boil, then remove from heat. Add salt and pepper to taste. Ladle into soup bowls, and garnish with dill leaves. Serve hot.

SERVES 6

EAST-WEST COLESLAW

What could be better for your next cross-cultural picnic?

4 large carrots, grated
½ green cabbage, shredded
3 scallions, thinly sliced on diagonal
2 tablespoons sesame seeds, toasted
¼ cup vegetable oil
1 tablespoon dark sesame oil
¼ cup rice wine vinegar
2 tablespoons soy sauce
2 tablespoons sugar
1 garlic clove, minced
1 teaspoon minced fresh ginger
salt and freshly ground pepper

In a large bowl, combine carrots, cabbage, scallions, and 1 tablespoon sesame seeds.

In a small bowl, whisk oils with vinegar, soy sauce, sugar, garlic, and ginger. Pour over salad, and toss to coat thoroughly. Season to taste with salt and pepper. Sprinkle with the remaining sesame seeds just before serving, or store in the refrigerator.

SERVES 6 TO 8

Purchasing

Choose brightly colored, plump, crisp carrots that are smooth and shiny with fresh green tops. Avoid carrots that are wilted, shriveled, moldy, or with greenish coloring or sprouts. Don't be fooled by plastic bags striped with orange.

THAI CARROT AND RICE SALAD

Here's a great, refreshing dish to bring to a summer potluck.

4 cups cooked and cooled jasmine rice
2 cups grated carrots
1 cucumber, seeded and sliced
¼ cup diced red onion
¼ cup chopped fresh mint
½ cup freshly squeezed lime juice
½ teaspoon grated lime zest
½ teaspoon red pepper flakes
½ cup peanut oil
red leaf lettuce leaves

In a large bowl, combine rice, carrots, cucumber, onion, and mint.

In a small bowl, combine lime juice, zest, and pepper flakes. Whisk in oil. Pour over rice mixture, and toss thoroughly. Serve over lettuce leaves arranged on serving plates.

SERVES 6 TO 8

Storing

Trimmed carrots can be stored in their original plastic bag in the refrigerator's coldest part or the vegetable crisper. If carrots were purchased loose, trim the green tops down to an inch or so and store them in a perforated plastic vegetable bag. If you plan on using the tops, store them in a separate bag. Mature carrots should keep for several weeks, while younger ones should be used within one week.

RUSSIAN SALAD

Not many salads can be prepared ahead of time like this classic carrot and potato salad.

4 carrots, cut in thirds
2 medium white boiling potatoes, peeled and
    quartered
1 cup frozen peas, thawed
½ cup mayonnaise
¼ cup ketchup
3 tablespoons chopped sweet pickle
1 tablespoon capers
romaine lettuce or radicchio leaves
salt and freshly ground pepper

In a small stockpot, cook carrots and potatoes in boiling salted water to cover until tender, about 15 minutes. Drain and cut into ⅜-inch dice. Place in large bowl, and add peas.

In a small bowl, whisk mayonnaise with ketchup, pickle, and capers. Add to vegetables and toss lightly but thoroughly. Refrigerate up to two days.

To serve, arrange lettuce leaves on a platter or individual plates. Season to taste with salt and pepper. Mound salad on top.

SERVES 6

Carrot Varieties
The carrot most of us know best is the Imperator, long and slightly tapered. But in some stores and at farm stands you can find the more cylindrical, stump-rooted Nantes variety and the sweet Chantenay—a large, thick, bright orange cone. The latter makes a wonderful bright and sweet juice.

MOROCCAN CARROT SALAD

Harissa, the fiery red pepper paste sold in tubes, can be found in specialty stores. You can raise the heat in this spicy dressing by adding harissa to taste.

1 pound carrots, grated
2 tablespoons chopped fresh parsley
3 garlic cloves, minced
¼ cup olive oil
grated zest and juice of 1 lemon
½ teaspoon harissa sauce or chile oil, or more
    to taste
salt and freshly ground pepper
additional chopped fresh parsley and green
    olives for garnish

In a bowl, combine carrots, parsley, and garlic.

In a separate bowl, whisk oil with lemon zest, juice, and harissa. Pour over carrot mixture, and toss thoroughly. Season to taste with salt and pepper. Serve at room temperature, sprinkled with parsley and garnished with olives.

SERVES 6

Away from the Horse's Mouth
Moving a horse who is stubborn as a mule is as easy as dangling a carrot from a stick attached to the beast's neck and just out of reach of its teeth.

CARROT AND CELERY ROOT SALAD

For those who really love their root vegetables: a double root salad!

1 medium celery root, julienned
juice of 1 lemon
4 large carrots, julienned
½ cup mayonnaise
¼ cup crème fraîche
2 tablespoons Dijon mustard
salt and freshly ground pepper
chopped chives for garnish

Place celery root in a large bowl. Add lemon juice, and toss to coat. Add carrots, and toss to combine.

In a small bowl, whisk mayonnaise with crème fraîche and mustard. Add to vegetables, and toss to coat. Season to taste with salt and pepper. Serve sprinkled with chives.

SERVES 6

Eat Your Sugars
Among vegetables, carrots are second only to beets in sugar content.

APPLE CARROT SALAD

This simple summer salad should be served immediately for maximum crunch and color.

3 large carrots, peeled
2 unpeeled Red Delicious apples
2 tablespoons lemon juice
1 teaspoon honey, or to taste

Grate or shred the carrots and apples, either by hand or by using the medium shredding disk on a food processor. Transfer to a large bowl. In a separate bowl, whisk together the lemon juice and honey. Pour over salad, and toss well to combine. Serve or chill for later.

MAKES 1 QUART

VIETNAMESE PICKLED CARROT SALAD

This classic, easy salad is nice served alongside grilled salmon or light sandwiches.

1 cup cold water
1 tablespoon sugar
1 tablespoon rice wine vinegar
¼ teaspoon salt
2 large carrots, peeled and finely shredded
4-inch-long daikon radish, peeled and finely
    shredded

In a bowl, stir together the water, sugar, vinegar, and salt until the sugar dissolves. Add carrot and radish, and stir well. Cover, and marinate in the refrigerator at least 1 hour or as long as a day. Drain and serve.

MAKES 1½ CUPS

Nutrition

Carrots are a mother lode of beta-carotene, a precursor of vitamin A. According to the *Berkeley Wellness Encyclopedia of Food and Nutrition*, a carrot-and-a-third provides more than five times the Recommended Daily Allowance of vitamin A, a nutritional bargain at a cost of 43 calories. Carrots also provide some vitamin C and are a good source of fiber.

Since carrots are tough-skinned, eating them in the raw (the vegetable, not you) may not be the best way to get most of the food value they have to offer. Cooking them just until tender-crisp makes their nutrients more accessible. However, overcooking can decrease carotene levels significantly.

CARROTY
SIDES

SWEET AND SOUR CARROT CHUTNEY

Good with grilled chicken, roasted lamb, curries, or cheese and crackers.

1 pound carrots, peeled and minced
1 large onion, thinly sliced
grated zest and juice of 4 oranges
2 Granny Smith apples, peeled, cored, and
    grated
½ cup currants
1 cup brown sugar
3 whole cloves
½ teaspoon cayenne pepper
1½ cups cider vinegar

In a large pot, combine carrots, onion, orange zest and juice, apples, currants, sugar, cloves, and cayenne. Pour in vinegar, and stir to blend. Bring to a boil, then reduce heat, cover, and simmer 45 minutes, stirring occasionally. Uncover and simmer 45 minutes longer, stirring occasionally, until mixture becomes thick. Chill. Store in the refrigerator up to two weeks.

MAKES ABOUT 1 QUART

"Large, naked, raw carrots are acceptable as food only to those who live in hutches eagerly awaiting Easter."
—Fran Lebowitz

SMASHED CARROTS
AND TURNIPS

*Here's a cozy dish to serve as part of a hearty
winter dinner.*

3 medium turnips, peeled and quartered
6 medium carrots, peeled and cut in 3-inch
   chunks
4 tablespoons (½ stick) butter
⅓ cup crème fraîche or sour cream
salt and freshly ground pepper

In a large pot, cook turnips in boiling salted water to cover, 15 minutes. Add carrots, and cook 15 minutes longer, or until vegetables are tender. Drain and return vegetables to the pot. Add butter and crème fraîche, and mash until almost smooth but with some lumps. Season to taste with salt and pepper.

SERVES 4

Carrot Perm

To make carrot curls for garnishing, dissolve ¼ cup of sugar in 2 cups of water, and chill. Shave thin strips from a large carrot, using a vegetable peeler. Trim the edges for even width, and cut ends on diagonal. Roll strips up and place in the compartments of an ice cube tray. Fill tray with sugar water, and chill for several hours. Defrost, and voilá!

ORANGE GLAZED CARROTS

If you don't have the time for matchsticks, just slice the carrots into ¼-inch rounds.

8 medium carrots, peeled and cut into matchsticks
¼ cup orange juice
2 tablespoons brown sugar
4 tablespoons (½ stick) butter
⅛ teaspoon ground cloves
salt and freshly ground pepper
chopped fresh parsley

Place carrots in a small saucepan, and add just enough water to cover. Bring to a boil, reduce to a simmer, and cook until tender, about 8 minutes.

Meanwhile, in a small skillet, combine orange juice, sugar, butter, and cloves. Stir over medium heat just until sugar dissolves. Drain carrots and add to the skillet. Season to taste with salt, pepper and parsley. Briefly cook over low heat, tossing to coat.

SERVES 6

Uses

Endless: raw, blanched, simmered, steamed, stewed, roasted, stir-fried, deep-fried, microwaved, or candied....sliced, sticked, grated, diced, chunked, curled, juiced, mashed, or puréed....

INDIAN SPICED CARROTS

The intense flavor and color of this dish make it a good partner for simple grilled fish.

4 tablespoons (½ stick) butter
1 pound carrots, sliced ½-inch thick
1 teaspoon crushed fennel seeds
½ teaspoon ground cumin
½ teaspoon ground coriander
¼ teaspoon turmeric
¼ teaspoon cayenne pepper
¼ cup water
salt
chopped fresh cilantro for garnish

In a large skillet, melt butter over medium-high heat. Sauté carrots about 5 minutes. Stir in fennel seeds, cumin, coriander, turmeric, cayenne, and water. Cover and simmer until carrots are tender and water is absorbed, about 8 minutes. Season to taste with salt. Sprinkle with cilantro, and serve warm.

SERVES 4

"The only carrots that interest me are the number you get in a diamond."

—*Mae West*

ROASTED BABY CARROTS AND ONIONS

Inspiration for this great winter accompaniment came from the first cooking class Karen attended, long before baby carrots became available in most markets.

¼ pound salt pork or bacon, diced
1 (14-ounce) package baby carrots
½ pound pearl onions, peeled, with an X cut
   in root ends
salt and freshly ground pepper

Preheat oven to 450 degrees F.

In a large, heavy skillet with an ovenproof handle, fry salt pork or bacon to render fat. Add carrots and onions, and sauté 1 minute. Place the skillet in the oven, and roast vegetables 10 to 15 minutes or until well browned and tender. Season with salt and pepper to taste.

SERVES 4

Cholesterol Count

According to a USDA study, eating carrots may lower blood cholesterol levels. Those who ate 7 ounces of carrots daily for three weeks had an average 11 percent reduction of cholesterol levels, probably due to calcium pectate, a fiber found in carrots.

PANFRIED BABY CARROTS AND POTATOES

This is an old family favorite of Karen's, slightly remodeled.

1 pound baby carrots, tops trimmed to 1 inch
1 pound baby yellow potatoes, cut in half
4 tablespoons (½ stick) butter
2 ounces pancetta or lean bacon
4 shallots, chopped
½ cup soft bread crumbs
1 tablespoon chopped fresh parsley
salt and freshly ground pepper

Combine carrots and potatoes in a steamer, and set over simmering water. Cover and steam until barely tender, 5 to 15 minutes, depending on size.

Meanwhile, in a skillet, melt 2 tablespoons butter over medium-high heat. Add pancetta, and fry until almost crisp. Add shallots, and cook until shallots are tender and pancetta is crisp. Stir in bread crumbs, and cook 2 minutes longer, stirring frequently. Stir in parsley, and season with salt and pepper to taste. Transfer to a platter and set aside.

In the same skillet, melt remaining butter over medium-high heat. Add carrots and potatoes, and cook, stirring occasionally, until they begin to brown, about 3 minutes. Transfer to a serving dish, top with pancetta mixture, and serve hot.

SERVES 4 TO 6

HONEYED CARROTS

Serve these sweet and crunchy stir-fried veggies over rice and alongside chicken for a quick, healthful dinner.

½ cup orange juice
¼ cup honey
2 tablespoons soy sauce
2 teaspoons cornstarch
2 tablespoons peanut or vegetable oil
4 large carrots, thinly sliced on diagonal
2 celery stalks, thinly sliced on diagonal
1 green bell pepper, cored, seeded, and cut in
    1½-inch squares
2 garlic cloves, minced
2 teaspoons minced fresh ginger
½ cup peanuts or cashews (optional)

In a small bowl, combine orange juice, honey, soy sauce, and cornstarch.

In a wok or large skillet, heat oil over high heat. Add carrots, and stir-fry 1 minute. Add celery and green peppers, and stir-fry 1 minute longer. Add garlic and ginger, and cook 30 seconds longer. Swirl orange juice mixture, and add to pan. Stir until thickened and clear, about 30 seconds. Stir in nuts, if desired.

SERVES 4

Overdose

If your nose turns yellow, you might be munching too many carrots. A high intake of carotenoid pigments, which give carrots their orange color, causes carotenemia, a harmless condition that disappears within a few weeks if carrot consumption is reduced. Makes one wonder why a bunny's nose is pink.

SWEET AND SOUR CARROTS

The carrot's natural sweetness is highlighted in this simple Italian treatment—delicious hot or cold.

2 pounds carrots, julienned
½ tablespoon olive oil
2 garlic cloves, minced
½ cup red wine vinegar
½ teaspoon sugar
½ teaspoon red pepper flakes
2 tablespoons chopped fresh oregano

Place the carrots in a microwave container, add a spoon or two of water, and cover with plastic wrap. Microwave on high 2 minutes. Drain.

Heat the oil in a large skillet over medium-high heat. Sauté garlic about 1 minute. Add carrots, and continue cooking, stirring frequently, about 2 minutes. Add vinegar, sugar, pepper flakes, and oregano. Continue cooking over high heat until the liquid has evaporated. Transfer to a platter, and serve hot or at room temperature.

SERVES 6

"Fifty million rabbits can't be wrong."
    —*Bruce Beck,* Produce, a Fruit and Vegetable Lovers' Guide

To Peel or Not to Peel

To get the most nutritional value and flavor out of carrots, you can cook them unpeeled (whole or in chunks). The skins, however, are easily removed with a vegetable peeler. Most commercially grown carrots are treated with a pesticide to discourage the carrot fly. Because most of the pesticide remains in the skin, if you're concerned about residue, peel your carrots just before using them.

MAIN COURSE
CARROTS

CHICKEN, CARROT, AND POTATO CURRY

Heat up this curry as much as you want with additional cayenne.

2 tablespoons peanut or vegetable oil
6 skinless, boneless chicken thighs, cut in
   1½-inch pieces
1 onion, roughly chopped
6 large carrots, cut in 2-inch lengths
2 medium baking potatoes, peeled and cut
   in eighths
2 garlic cloves, minced
1 tablespoon minced fresh ginger
2 teaspoons curry powder
1 (13½-ounce) can unsweetened coconut milk
salt and cayenne pepper
hot cooked rice
chopped cilantro for garnish

In a large skillet, heat oil over medium-high heat. Add chicken, and cook, turning frequently, until browned all over, about 5 minutes. With a slotted spoon, remove chicken and set aside. Add onion, carrots, potatoes, garlic, and ginger, and sauté just until vegetables begin to brown, about 3 minutes. Add curry powder, and cook 1 minute longer.

Return chicken to pan, and add coconut milk. Bring to a boil, reduce heat to a simmer, and cook uncovered, stirring occasionally, about 15 minutes or until vegetables are tender. Season with salt and cayenne to taste. Serve over rice, and sprinkle with cilantro.

SERVES 4

IRISH STEW

Lamb lovers won't want to wait for St. Patrick's Day for this satisfying stew.

1½ pounds boneless lamb shoulder, cut in
    1-inch cubes
salt and freshly ground pepper
¼ cup flour
4 tablespoons (½ stick) butter
1 pound baby carrots
1 pound baby red potatoes, cut in half
½ pound pearl onions, peeled, an X cut in
    root ends
1 garlic clove, minced
1½ cups vegetable broth
1 teaspoon dried rosemary
1 teaspoon dried thyme
½ cup frozen peas

Season meat all over with salt and pepper. Evenly dredge meat in flour, reserving any leftover flour.

In a large pot, melt 2 tablespoons butter over medium-high heat. Add meat and cook until evenly browned, about 5 minutes. Remove meat, and set aside.

Melt remaining butter in pot. Add carrots, potatoes, onions, and garlic. Cook, stirring frequently, until vegetables are golden, about 6 minutes. Add remaining flour, and cook and stir 1 minute. Gradually stir in broth. Bring to a boil, stirring constantly. Continue to cook and stir just until sauce has thickened, about 3 minutes. Return meat to pot. Stir in rosemary and thyme, reduce heat, and simmer covered, 45 minutes, stirring occasionally. Stir in peas, and cook just until heated through. Serve hot.

SERVES 6

BRAISED SHORT RIBS WITH CARROTS

This hearty dish is reminiscent of the forties and fifties. Making it a day ahead improves the flavor.

2 tablespoons vegetable oil
2 pounds beef short ribs
1 large onion, roughly chopped
2 garlic cloves, minced
½ teaspoon dried rosemary
½ teaspoon dried thyme
1 cup water
3 cups ½-inch carrot slices
chopped fresh parsley for garnish

In a large, heavy pot, heat oil over medium-high heat. Add short ribs, and cook, turning several times, until well browned, about 5 minutes. Remove meat and set aside.

Add onion and garlic and sauté until soft, about 3 minutes. Return meat to pot, and add rosemary and thyme. Add 1 cup water, and bring to a boil. Reduce heat to low, cover, and simmer 1½ hours. Add carrots, and continue to simmer covered, about 15 minutes longer or until carrots are tender. Serve sprinkled with parsley.

SERVES 4

Zap 'em

To microwave a pound of carrots, cut them into 1-inch pieces and place in a microwave-safe bowl with 2 table-spoons water, broth, or fruit juice, such as orange or pineapple. Cover and microwave 4 to 6 minutes on high, stopping and stirring once or twice.

CARROT AND ONION TART

Purchase a prerolled pie crust in the refrigerated section of the grocery store, or make your favorite pie crust recipe.

1 refrigerated prerolled pie crust
2 tablespoons olive oil
1 cup thinly sliced onion
1 cup grated carrots
3 tablespoons chopped parsley
½ teaspoon dried thyme
1 cup milk
½ cup heavy cream
3 eggs
¾ cup grated Gruyère cheese
salt and freshly ground pepper, to taste

Preheat oven to 375 degrees F. Line a 9-inch tart pan with a removable bottom or a pie plate with the pie crust. Fold the edge under and pinch as desired. Chill.

In a large skillet, heat oil over medium-high heat. Sauté onion until golden, about 3 minutes. Stir in carrots, parsley, and thyme, and cook 1 minute longer. Let cool slightly.

In a bowl, beat milk, cream, and eggs. Add cheese and salt and pepper. Spread vegetables evenly over the bottom of the chilled crust. Pour milk mixture over vegetables. Bake about 45 minutes, until set. Cool slightly or to room temperature before serving.

SERVES 6

Namesake

Carotenoids—the yellow and orange pigments in plants, including beta-carotene—are so named because they were first identified in carrots.

RISOTTO WITH CARROTS AND PEAS

Peas and carrots never had it so good.

4 tablespoons (½ stick) butter
1 medium onion, diced
3 medium carrots, peeled and diced
1½ cups arborio or short-grain rice
8 cups reduced-salt chicken or vegetable
    broth, heated
¼ cup white wine
⅓ cup grated Parmesan cheese
½ cup frozen petite peas
salt and pepper
chopped fresh parsley
additional grated Parmesan cheese

In a large, heavy saucepan, melt 2 tablespoons butter over medium-high heat. Add onion, and cook, stirring frequently, until translucent, about 3 minutes. Add carrots, and cook 2 minutes longer. Stir in rice. Reduce heat, and cook about 3 minutes, stirring frequently, until rice begins to turn translucent.

Turn up heat, and ladle in about ½ cup hot broth, stirring until almost evaporated. Add enough additional broth to cover the rice. Reduce heat and simmer, stirring frequently, until the broth is nearly absorbed. Continue adding broth, about ½ cup at a time, stirring frequently after each addition, until the rice is almost done but still crunchy. Stir in wine, and cook 5 minutes longer. If rice is not done, add more broth, ¼ cup at a time, continually stirring, until done. Rice should be creamy, not fluffy. Stir in cheese and peas, and cook until peas are heated. Season to taste with salt and pepper. Sprinkle with parsley, and pass additional cheese at the table.

SERVES 6

MOROCCAN CHICKEN
WITH COUSCOUS

Harissa sauce, a blend of olive oil, garlic, hot chiles, and spices, can be purchased at Middle Eastern grocery stores. Or you may substitute chile oil or red pepper flakes to taste.

2 tablespoons olive oil
3 pounds chicken pieces
1 pound carrots, cut in 3-inch lengths
2 onions, cut in eighths
2 teaspoons ground cumin
1 teaspoon each ground coriander,
    cinnamon, cloves, and ginger
a few saffron threads
4 zucchini, cut in 3-inch lengths
1 teaspoon harissa sauce
1 (10-ounce) package couscous

In a large pot, heat oil over medium-high heat. Add chicken, and sauté, turning several times, until golden all over. Remove chicken and set aside. Add carrots and onions to the pan, and cook, stirring occasionally, until lightly browned. Return chicken to the pot along with spices. Add just enough water to cover. Bring to a boil, reduce the heat to a simmer, and cook covered, 30 minutes.

Add zucchini, and cook about 5 minutes longer, or until zucchini is tender and chicken is cooked through. With a slotted spoon, remove chicken and vegetables from the broth, and transfer to a large dish and keep warm. Transfer 1½ cups broth to a small pan set over medium heat (reserve remaining broth for couscous). Stir in harissa, and bring to a boil. Reduce heat, and simmer 10 minutes to reduce slightly.

Meanwhile, cook couscous according to the package directions, using the remaining broth for part of the cooking liquid.

To serve, pile couscous on a platter or on individual plates, top with chicken and vegetables, and drizzle with sauce. Pass remaining sauce at the table.

SERVES 4 TO 6

SEA BASS, CARROTS, AND FENNEL IN PARCHMENT

Baking in paper yields a moist, low-fat dish, with concentrated flavors.

4 large carrots, peeled and julienned
1 small fennel bulb, julienned
½ green bell pepper, julienned
½ red bell pepper, julienned
2 tablespoons extra virgin olive oil
grated peel of 1 lemon
salt and freshly ground pepper
4 (6- to 8-ounce) sea bass fillets
sprigs of fennel tops

Preheat oven to 425 degrees F.

From parchment paper or foil, cut out four heart shapes measuring about 14 inches from top to bottom at center. Butter one side of each heart.

In a medium bowl, combine carrots, fennel, peppers, oil, and lemon peel. Salt and pepper to taste.

Place one piece of fish in the center of one half of each heart. Place one-quarter of the vegetable mixture over and around each fillet. Fold the parchment over the fish and vegetables so that paper edges are even. Starting at the top edge of each heart, fold and crimp paper edges together to seal each packet. Place on baking sheet, and bake 15 minutes.

To serve, place each packet on an individual plate and cut an X in the top of each with scissors. Curl paper edges back to open, and garnish with fennel sprigs. Serve hot.

SERVES 4

"Vegetables are a must on a diet. I suggest carrot cake."
    —*Jim Davis,* Garfield

Carrot Evolution

In the beginning, carrots grew wild in Afghanistan in bright hues of yellow or purple, fugitives of the Umbelliferae family, whose matriarch may have been Queen Anne's lace. In the Middle Ages, the Dutch grew the first orange carrots. Now, tamed after more than 2,000 years of breeding, most of the 400 commercially grown varieties are bright orange.

At supermarkets, we mostly purchase the familiar long, tapered Imperator variety. Baby carrots have become more available during the past decade, but only the ones sold loose with their feathery tops are true babies; those sold in water packs are often mature carrots that have been carved down. Water-packed carrots sold in convenient stick and grated forms may have lost some of their flavor and nutritional value in the process.

Now that visits to farmers markets are a pastime many of us can enjoy again, globe- and cone-shaped carrots, from finger- to arm-size, can be found. One California farmer is growing carrots in white, yellow, and purple colors reminiscent of the original varieties.

CARROT SWEETS
AND
BEVERAGES

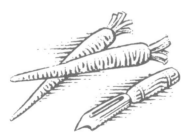

GINGERED CARROT PIE

This sweet, rich, orange-tinted pie is a great variation on the pumpkin pie theme for Thanksgiving.

1 pound carrots, cut in 3-inch lengths
1 refrigerated prerolled pie crust
1 cup applesauce
¼ cup brown sugar
3 eggs
1 cup evaporated milk
2 tablespoons chopped crystallized ginger
1½ teaspoons pumpkin or apple pie spice
grated zest of 1 lemon

Preheat oven to 350 degrees F.

In the top of a steamer or on a rack set over simmering water, steam carrots 10 to 15 minutes until very tender. Cool slightly.

Line a 9-inch pie plate with crust. Turn edge under and crimp as desired.

Place steamed carrots in a food processor or blender and process until puréed. Add applesauce, brown sugar, eggs, evaporated milk, 1½ tablespoons ginger, pie spice, and lemon zest. Process until blended. Pour into prepared pie crust, sprinkle with remaining ginger, and bake 40 to 45 minutes or until center is just set. Cool on wire rack.

SERVES 8

"We shall continue to operate on the Italian donkey at both ends, with a carrot and a stick."

—Winston Churchill, campaign speech, May 1943

24-KARAT CARROT CAKE

The name speaks for itself—the classic all-American carrot cake.

CAKE
2 cups cake flour
2 teaspoons baking powder
1½ teaspoons baking soda
1 teaspoon salt
2 teaspoons cinnamon
4 eggs
1 cup brown sugar
1 cup granulated sugar
1½ cups vegetable oil
3 cups grated carrots
¾ cup roughly chopped walnuts or pecans

CREAM CHEESE FROSTING
8 tablespoons (1 stick) butter, room temperature
8 ounces cream cheese, room temperature
1½ teaspoons vanilla
1 pound confectioners' sugar, sifted

Preheat the oven to 350 degrees F. Butter and flour a 13- x 9-inch cake pan.

In a mixing bowl, sift together flour, baking powder, baking soda, salt, and cinnamon.

In a separate bowl, beat eggs, sugars, and oil until creamy. Beat in the dry ingredients to blend. Stir in carrots and nuts. Transfer to the prepared pan, and bake 45 to 55 minutes or until cake springs back when touched lightly. Cool in pan on wire rack.

For the frosting, beat together the butter, cream cheese, vanilla, and sugar until smooth.

Turn cake out, and spread frosting over top and sides. Cut into squares to serve.

SERVES 12 TO 15

CARROT CURRANT OATMEAL DROPS

Bet these are gone before they are cool enough to drop in the cookie jar.

1 cup flour
½ teaspoon baking powder
½ teaspoon baking soda
½ teaspoon cinnamon
½ teaspoon salt
⅓ cup vegetable oil
1 cup brown sugar
1 egg
1½ cups rolled oats
1½ cups grated, peeled carrots
½ cup currants
2 tablespoons grated orange zest

Preheat oven to 375 degrees F. Butter two baking sheets.

In a mixing bowl, sift together flour, baking powder, baking soda, cinnamon, and salt.

In the bowl of an electric mixer, beat oil with brown sugar and egg until blended. Add the dry ingredients, and mix to blend. Stir in oats, carrots, currants, and orange zest. Drop by tablespoonfuls, about 2 inches apart, onto prepared baking sheets. Bake about 10 minutes or until golden. Remove from baking sheets, and cool on wire racks.

MAKES ABOUT 2 DOZEN DROPS

"Ladies of the Stuart court pinned the feathery plumage of young carrots to their heads and on their splendid hats."

—*Jane Grigson*, The Vegetable Book

CARROT MAPLE PUDDING À LA MODE

If you close your eyes, you'll think you're in Vermont.

- ¾ cup flour
- ¾ teaspoon baking powder
- ½ teaspoon baking soda
- 1 teaspoon pumpkin pie spice
- 6 tablespoons (¾ stick) butter
- ¾ cup maple syrup
- 3 eggs
- 1½ cups finely grated carrots
- grated zest of 1 large orange
- coarse raw sugar
- 1 pint vanilla ice cream

Preheat oven to 350 degrees F. Butter a 1-quart shallow casserole dish. Butter one side of foil square large enough to cover dish.

Sift together flour, baking powder, baking soda, and pie spice in a mixing bowl.

In a separate bowl, cream butter with maple syrup until well blended. Beat in eggs, one at a time. Stir in the dry ingredients. Fold in carrots and orange zest. Transfer to the prepared dish, and set in larger baking pan. Pour in enough hot water to come halfway up sides of casserole. Cover pudding with prepared foil, buttered-side down. Bake 30 minutes. Remove foil, sprinkle with raw sugar, and continue baking until pudding springs back when lightly touched, about 20 minutes longer. Cool slightly, and serve warm with ice cream.

SERVES 6

Rx for Fighter Pilots
During World War II, to improve the night vision of fighter pilots, carrot breeders in Britain successfully doubled the carotene content of carrots to be eaten by RAF aviators.

CARROT APRICOT CAKE

The inspiration for this easy, hand-mixed carrot cake came from French chef Roger Verge. Dress it up with whipped cream if you feel indulgent.

½ cup dried apricots, chopped
⅔ cup flour
½ cup brown sugar
1½ teaspoons baking powder
½ teaspoon salt
4 eggs
¼ cup vegetable oil
1 teaspoon vanilla
1 teaspoon grated fresh ginger
2 teaspoons grated lemon zest
1 large or 2 small carrots, trimmed, peeled, and thickly sliced

Combine the chopped apricots in a small bowl with hot water to cover. Let sit 20 minutes to soften.

Preheat oven to 350 degrees F. Coat an 8-inch round cake pan with oil, and line with parchment.

In a large mixing bowl, stir together flour, brown sugar, baking powder, and salt. Whisk in eggs, oil, vanilla, ginger, and lemon zest until blended thoroughly. Stir in carrots. Drain apricots and stir into batter. Pour batter into the prepared pan. Bake 30 to 35 minutes, until a tester inserted in the center comes out clean. Cool in the pan on a rack for 10 minutes. Invert onto rack, and peel the paper. Cool completely before serving.

SERVES 8

CARROT RAISIN WAFFLES

These full-flavored, moist waffles are good, and healthful enough to eat for dinner. Just skip the syrup and top with plain yogurt and more raisins.

1 cup milk
2 eggs
3 tablespoons butter, melted
¼ cup raisins
¾ cup flour
¼ cup sugar
2½ teaspoons baking powder
¼ teaspoon salt
½ teaspoon cinnamon
¼ teaspoon ground nutmeg
¼ cup finely chopped walnuts
½ cup finely shredded carrots

Preheat the waffle iron. Whisk together milk, eggs, butter, and raisins, and set aside 15 minutes to plump.

In a large mixing bowl, combine flour, sugar, baking powder, salt, cinnamon, and nutmeg. Mix with a fork. Pour milk mixture into flour, and stir to combine. Gently stir in nuts and carrots.

Pour onto the waffle maker and follow the manufacturer's instructions. Serve with maple syrup or a dollop of plain yogurt, sprinkled with raisins and honey.

SERVES 4

Keeping Company with Carrots
Carrots do well with nutmeg, ginger, cinnamon, fennel (fresh or crushed seeds), dill, mint, cabbage, peas, celery, onion, other root vegetables, butter, sweet or sour cream, yogurt, citrus juices and peel, raisins, brown sugar, honey, maple syrup, and just about any meat, fish, or poultry.

CARROT COGNAC FLIPS

The egg whites are warmed prior to mixing as a precaution against the slim possibility of salmonella contamination.

2 egg whites
½ cup carrot juice
½ cup half-and-half
¼ cup Cognac, brandy, bourbon, or
    orange juice
crushed ice
nutmeg
carrot curls or orange slices

In a skillet, heat 1 inch of water to simmering. Turn off heat.

In a medium metal bowl, stir egg whites until they are just broken up. Set bowl in the skillet of water and stir with a rubber spatula, scraping the bottom and sides of the bowl constantly, until whites reach 160 degrees F, about 1 minute.

In a cocktail shaker or bowl, combine carrot juice, half-and-half, egg whites, and Cognac. Add a handful of crushed ice, and shake thoroughly. Strain into two (8-ounce) cocktail glasses. Sprinkle with nutmeg, and garnish with carrot curls or orange slices.

SERVES 2

STICKY BRAN MUFFINS

These are so gooey you might want to use a fork.

4 tablespoons (½ stick) butter
6 tablespoons brown sugar
1 cup granulated sugar
6 tablespoons honey
1 tablespoon water
1 cup flour
½ teaspoon baking soda
½ teaspoon cinnamon
½ teaspoon salt
3 cups whole bran
2 eggs
¼ cup vegetable oil
1½ cups buttermilk
1 cup grated carrots
1 cup chopped pecans
½ cup golden raisins

Preheat oven to 400 degrees F.

In the bowl of an electric mixer, cream butter until fluffy. Beat in brown sugar and ⅓ cup of the granulated sugar. Add 2 tablespoons of honey and the water, and beat until light. Coat eighteen muffin cups equally with sugar mixture.

In a separate large bowl, sift together flour, baking soda, cinnamon, and salt.

Place the bran in a medium bowl. Whisk in the eggs, remaining honey, and oil. Stir in buttermilk. Stir liquid mixture into dry ingredients just until blended but still lumpy. Stir in carrots, pecans, and raisins. Fill prepared muffin cups three-quarters full. Bake 20 minutes. Invert muffin pans on wire racks to release muffins. Serve warm or at room temperature.

MAKES 18 MUFFINS

CARROT RAISIN MUFFINS

These moist, spicy muffins will chase any overly sweet, leaden carrot experiences from your memory bank.

2 eggs
½ cup plus 2 tablespoons vegetable oil
½ cup sugar
1½ cups coarsely grated carrot
½ cup raisins
¾ cup walnuts, toasted and chopped
1½ cups all-purpose flour
2¼ teaspoons baking powder
¼ teaspoon salt
1½ teaspoons cinnamon
½ teaspoon nutmeg

Preheat oven to 400 degrees F. Grease or line muffin tins with paper cups.

In a large mixing bowl, whisk eggs, oil, and sugar until smooth. Stir in carrots, raisins, and ½ cup of the nuts.

In another bowl, stir together remaining ingredients except nuts. Add flour mixture to carrot mixture and stir well to combine. (The batter will be stiff.)

Spoon into muffin cups and sprinkle tops with remaining nuts. Bake about 25 minutes, until a tester comes out clean.

MAKES 10 MUFFINS

CARROT SMOOTHIE

Who needs mango-kiwi-blueberry-guava?

1 cup carrot juice
1 banana
1 cup plain or maple yogurt
½ cup ice cubes

Place juice, banana, yogurt, and ice in blender.
Process until smooth and thick. Serve cold.

SERVES 2 (12 OUNCES EACH)

Haiku to a Carrot
Carrot, earth-yanked root,
salad's punctuation,
commas in a cake.
        —*Sara Gillingham*

CONVERSIONS

LIQUID
1 Tbsp = 15 ml
½ cup = 4 fl oz = 125 ml
1 cup = 8 fl oz = 250 ml

DRY
¼ cup = 4 Tbsp = 2 oz = 60 g
1 cup = ½ pound = 8 oz = 250 g

FLOUR
½ cup = 60 g
1 cup = 4 oz = 125 g

TEMPERATURE
400° F = 200° C = gas mark 6
375° F = 190° C = gas mark 5
350° F = 175° C = gas mark 4

MISCELLANEOUS
2 Tbsp butter = 1 oz = 30 g
1 inch = 2.5 cm
all-purpose flour = plain flour
baking soda = bicarbonate of soda
brown sugar = demerara sugar
heavy cream = double cream
sugar = caster sugar